LET'S LOOK AT

Arms and Armour

LET'S LOOK AT

Arms and Armour

by

F. Wilkinson

Illustrated by

Laurence V. Archer

Scholastic Publications

First published in Great Britain 1968 by
Frederick Muller Ltd.

This edition published 1975 by Scholastic Publications Ltd,
161 Fulham Road, London SW3 6SW

To Joanna
The author would like to express his thanks to C. Blair, M.A., F.S.A.,
for reading the manuscript and making several helpful suggestions

Printed by Sir Joseph Causton and Son Ltd,
London and Eastleigh

LET'S LOOK AT

Arms and Armour

Assyrian helmets

A motor-cyclist wears a crash-helmet, a miner also wears a helmet—a cricketer wears pads and a footballer wears boots with specially strengthened toe-caps. Whenever there is danger of injury people wear some kind of protective clothing. The greater the danger the more important it becomes to have plenty of protection. War, one of man's most dangerous occupations, demanded most protection and to guard himself he made armour.

Primitive man soon discovered that a blow on the head was especially dangerous and one of the oldest pieces of armour that we find is a helmet, although the shield was probably the first of man's protective equipment. Shields of wood or leather, and helmets appear in the carvings and paintings of the Assyrians, Sumerians and Egyptians. The first helmets were probably tough leather caps, but as man discovered the secrets of making copper, bronze and, later, iron, he began to make metal helmets. Wooden shields were also strengthened or reinforced with strips of metal along the edges and at the centre.

As the smiths became more proficient and able to produce a good supply of metal the soldiers demanded that they use their skill to provide more efficient protection. One of the easiest ways was to attach small overlapping plates of metal or horn to a tunic and this was known as scale armour. It was flexible and easy to make and, in various forms, remained popular for many centuries, indeed, modern bullet-proof waistcoats are still made in much the same way. Pictures of Assyrian warriors show them wearing long tunics of scale armour which reached down to their ankles.

The Greeks were very skilful metal-workers, able to make scale armour and fashion large plates of bronze and mould them into shapes. Their body armour (*cuirass*) was made of two pieces—the breastplate, often moulded to resemble the muscles of the body, at the front and a thinner backplate. They buckled together at the side. *Greaves* protected the shins and were made of springy metal which gripped the leg to hold the armour in place. Upon his head the Greek warrior wore a

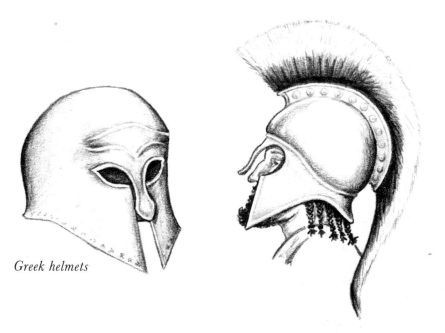

Greek helmets

strong helmet of bronze often made so that the entire face was covered except for two keyhole-shaped slits which left his eyes clear. In battle the helmet was decorated with a crest which might be in the form of an animal or perhaps great tufts or plumes of coloured horsehair. Not only did the crest make the warrior look tall and fierce, but it also helped his friends, and enemies, to pick him out from the crowd. For extra protection the Greek carried a great shield of leather and wood which was

Assyrian

Greek

either round or rather like the shape of a violin body. An arrangement of straps enabled the soldier to carry his shield slung on his back or held firmly on the left arm. Swords and spears were the most usual weapons, but bows and arrows, clubs, slings, and chariots also formed part of his armoury. Homer's tales are full of stories of great battles between heroes using all these weapons. Officers of the Roman Army wore a cuirass rather like the moulded Greek breastplate and back-plate as well as a helmet decorated with plumes of horsehair.

The Roman army was divided into legions, each of anything from four to six thousand men, and these were divided into ten cohorts. Individual soldiers were known as legionaries. Upon his head the legionary wore a simple metal helmet with two flat peaks, one to guard his neck and the other to protect his face. Two shaped ear-flaps gave protection to the sides of his face and these were tied, with a thong, beneath his chin. Round his neck he carried a scarf-like cloth and over a thigh-length tunic he wore his armour. This might be scale armour with its dozens of overlapping plates, or it might be a mail shirt constructed of hundreds of interlocking rings. Mail was a very old type of armour dating back to the third century B.C. Perhaps most common of all was the *lorica segmentata* made up of bands of metal encircling the body and crossing over the shoulders. Stout, nail-studded sandals completed the legionary's clothing, but he also carried a large, rectangular, curved shield (*scutum*) which was strengthened with iron.

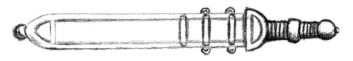

Roman sword

Roman legionary

In battle the legions were formed into lines facing the enemy and then, at the word of command, each soldier flung his javelin (*pilum*). This pilum was over six feet long and had an iron-shod wooden grip fitted with a long, soft iron shaft and point. If the pilum pierced an enemy shield the soft iron of the shaft bent and made it extremely difficult to pull out and so hindered the proper use of the shield giving the Roman an opportunity to finish off the enemy with his short sword (*gladius*). Since the gladius was fairly short it could be drawn with ease and was usually carried on the right side.

When the Roman Empire was collapsing in the fifth century Europe soon fell prey to attacks from the barbaric tribes of Goths, Franks, Saxons, Angles, Jutes and Vikings. Many of them had little or no armour, relying on their round wooden

Roman standard-bearer

Warrior from Gaul

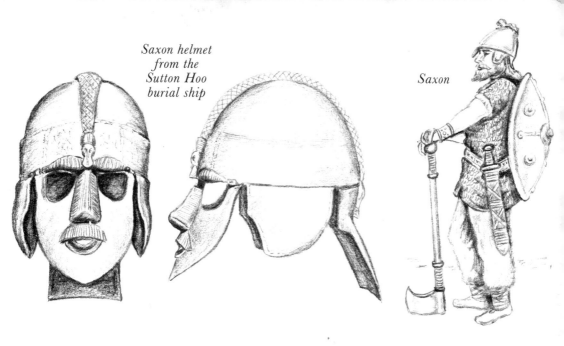

shields and long keen-edged spears and axes. Chiefs and leaders were better equipped with swords, helmets and coats of mail (*hauberks*) reaching to their knees. The helmets completely covered their heads leaving slits for the eyes and the face-pieces were decorated with silver inlay to represent eyebrows and moustaches. These fierce warriors slashed at their enemies with long two-edged swords and, unlike the Romans, seldom used the point of the three-foot-long-blade. As the blade was long and heavy it was balanced by putting a weight, called the *pommel*, at the top of the grip so making the weapon much easier to handle. Shields were usually round and were carried by slipping the arm through a loop and gripping a bar at the centre.

Some of the sea-rovers settled in Northern France and in time became known as the Normans, and it was from these ancestors that William the Conqueror was descended. Although very little Norman arms and armour has survived we do know quite a lot about their equipment for the Bayeux Tapestry shows many details. This famous Tapestry was probably made in England, but it tells the Norman story and the English are shown in Norman dress. The troops wear a coat of mail (it is incorrect to call it chain-mail) or hauberk, which reaches to the knee and is split front and back so that the knight may sit upon his horse. Sleeves are wide and cover only the upper arm. Although the Tapestry shows some figures to be naked under their hauberks it is almost certain that the knight wore some kind of tunic, for it would have been very uncomfortable and even painful without something to protect the skin from the links which would rub and pinch unless, of course, the inside of the hauberk was lined. Over their heads the Normans have a hood or *coif* of mail, sometimes separate and sometimes part of the hauberk. A few of the soldiers are shown with mail leggings or *chausses*.

Helmets were conical and had a bar or *nasal* which covered the nose and protected the wearer's face against a sword slash. As the Normans fought mostly on horseback their shields were long, kite-shaped and slightly concave so that they covered the mounted knight from his shoulder to his foot.

The swords were very much like those of their Viking ancestors with straight *quillons* (bar or guard for the hand, which was fitted across the tip of the blade below the grip) and a pommel shaped like a tea-cosy. Lances were fairly short and often carried a small flag or *gonfalon* just below the point. Against the Normans was the Saxon Army composed of foot soldiers, many without armour, although they are shown on the Tapestry in mail, and using swords, spears and long-handled axes. Most Saxon shields were round and strengthened with metal, and in battle the troops overlapped the edges of the shields to form an impenetrable shield wall. Over the top of the shield wall their long axes flashed and slashed and drove back the Norman charges again and again down the hill of

Norman knights

Senlac on that day in October 1066. If the shield wall had held steady the history of England would have been very different, but William broke the wall, Harold, King of the Saxons, was struck down, not by an arrow, but by Norman swords and England was William's.

Mail was to remain the commonest form of armour for the next two centuries, although scale armour was also used. Armourers used their great skill to provide better protection for the soldier by covering more of his body with mail. In the twelfth century a flap, or *ventail*, to cover the chin was introduced. Legs were now covered with strips of mail or by mail stockings supported from the waist. By the end of the twelfth century the sleeves of the hauberk were made long enough to cover the hands with a kind of mitten called a *muffler* which covered the back of the hand but left the palm clear so that the soldier could grip his sword or lance. Over all this mail the

Harold's last stand at Hastings

Sword hilts from the Bronze Age to the Viking Period

soldier wore a long loose tunic, called a *surcoat*, to keep off the sun which would otherwise have made the warrior even hotter and sweatier than he already was. Later these surcoats were decorated with the owner's coat of arms.

The conical helmet was in use until the end of the thirteenth century, but other types had a rounded top and towards the end of the twelfth century a flat-topped variety appeared. Many of these helmets were fitted with a guard which completely covered the face and was pierced only by breathing-holes and eye-slits. By about 1220 this face-guard had joined a neck-guard and formed a completely cylindrical helmet which later became the *great helm*. These heavy helmets were worn over a padded arming cap which helped to hold the helm firmly in place as well as reducing the shock of any blow. About the same time, the end of the twelfth century, we begin to find the introduction of crests fitted to the top of the helm. Probably of whalebone, leather or parchment, these crests were decorated with the badge of the wearer, for now his face and body were completely covered by his armour and it was necessary to have some means of recognition. This was the beginning of heraldry, for families began to use badges and crests that were recognised as belonging to them.

Most of the knights would have worn a great helm, but some, as well as most of the foot soldiers, wore a kettle hat which had a wide brim and looked rather like a soldier's steel helmet of the First World War.

In the latter part of the twelfth century it became common practice to wear a padded garment, or *aketon*, beneath the mail, for not only did this make for greater comfort, but it also gave extra protection. Indeed, some of these padded garments were used on their own as a form of simple and cheap armour. Shields had become smaller and were more like the base of an electric iron in shape.

Clad in his mail and aketon the knight was safe from all but the most severe blows and the greatest number of casualties in a battle was that of the poorly armed foot soldiers. Eye-witnesses tell us that during the Crusades knights could be seen looking like hedgehogs because of the arrows caught in their mail and yet they were still unscratched.

Archers of this period used either a short bow which was only drawn back as far as the chest and was not terribly power-ful, or the crossbow which was very powerful and, in many ways, easier to use. A springy bow was fitted at right angles to

European knights of the twelfth/thirteenth century

Thirteenth-century helmets

a bar or tiller and a thick, strong cord was pulled back until it slipped into a notched block which held it in that position. These bows were so strong that both hands were needed to pull back the cord, but as they became even stronger a hook was fastened to the belt and put under the cord so that the whole body could be used to pull it back. A stirrup was fixed at the end so that the foot could hold the weapon steady. A short arrow, known as a *quarrel* or *bolt*, was placed in a groove in front of the string and when ready the bowman pressed a lever which released the cord allowing it to fly forward discharging the bolt.

Mail was heavy and an average knight when fully armoured with aketon, mail, helmet and sword probably weighed about eighteen stone. A strong horse was required to carry a heavy load such as this, especially as the horse itself might be covered with a mail trapper. These big powerful horses were fairly slow and the Crusaders found it difficult to charge their Saracen foes since it took so long to get up speed that the Saracens had plenty of time to wheel their light-footed ponies out of the way of the lumbering Christian knights.

Mail formed a very good defence but it had certain drawbacks. It could only be made stronger by increasing the thickness of the links, but this meant that the mail became much too stiff and rigid and the wearer was unable to move easily. If the mail was split by a sword cut or lance thrust, the broken links

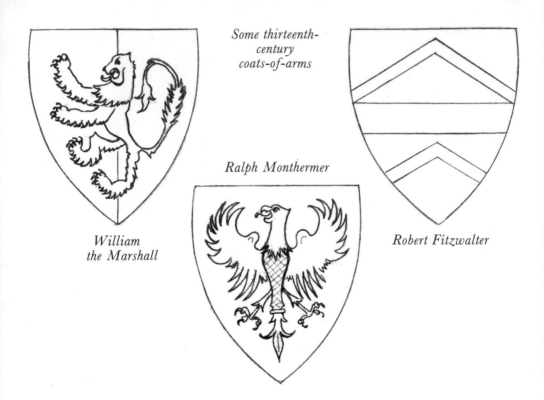

Some thirteenth-
century
coats-of-arms

*William
the Marshall*

Ralph Monthermer

Robert Fitzwalter

might be pushed into the open wound making it much worse. Armourers sought other ways to strengthen, or reinforce, the mail and one of the first materials they used was a specially treated leather known as *cuir bouilli* which was very tough but light. A cuirass or bodice of this leather was worn under the surcoat. The surcoat itself was often strengthened by riveting strips of metal plate on the inside.

The armourers also added reinforcing plates directly on to the mail, and from about 1250 we get the beginnings of plate armour. The first pieces appear about 1230–50 and were small plates, called *poleyns*, fitted to the knee. Gradually their size increased until, by about 1275, they cover the front and sides of the knee. Further protection to the leg was given by a length of plate, rather like a piece of gutter, which was fastened to the shin. Known as the *schynbald* they were worn either over, or under, the mail. Protection for the arms followed much the same pattern with the addition of *couters* or small plates at the elbow from about 1300.

A memorial to Sir William Fitzralph dating from about 1323 shows the next step for he now has two plates, one protecting the upper and another the lower arm, a couter at the elbow and two discs or *besagews* fixed at elbow and shoulder. Gauntlets of metal first appear at the end of the thirteenth century and they are rather like scale armour with a number of small metal plates attached to a glove. The body was also given extra protection by a coat of plates which appears to have been a leather or cloth tunic to which a number of metal plates were riveted. It was worn like the cuirass, over the hauberk.

A plate-metal defence for the neck and chin—the *bevor* or collar—also appears at the beginning of the fourteenth century and looks rather like a high stiff collar reaching to the mouth.

Details of the armour of this period are not very well understood for very few pieces have survived and all the information we have comes from paintings of the time, old records, statues and memorials. Effigies and brasses are two of the most

Cross bow

top view

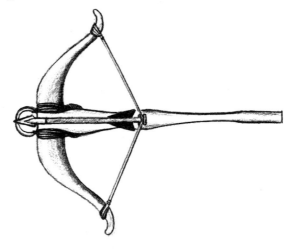

side view

valuable sources of information, for when a knight was buried his tomb was often marked with a full-sized carving—an effigy—or a large sheet of brass on which was engraved a likeness of him complete with all his armour. Fortunately, a number of these effigies and brasses have survived undamaged and can still be seen in our churches.

Saracen knight

Late twelfth/mid thirteenth century knights

What did a knight of about 1325 wear when he rode into battle? By this time nearly all the body was protected by mail and plate but, of course, this does not mean that every knight wore exactly the same armour. Some were too poor to get the latest styles whilst others were satisfied with their old familiar mail, so let us imagine that our knight has the very latest style of armour. First he puts on a fairly close-fitting shirt and a pair of stout breeches and woollen stockings or hose. Now he pulls on the leggings of mail, *chausses*, to which the poleyns or knee-plates are fixed. Next come some extra quilted thigh-pieces or *cuisses*. These quilted or *gamboised cuisses* were worn either over or under the mail according to taste. Next the greaves, for by now plates were made to fit right round the lower legs. *Sabatons*, or shoes, of leather covered with metal plates, or perhaps strips or *lames*, were next to be put on and lastly came the spurs. Now the aketon, first of the body-pieces, was put on and over this went the mail hauberk. Our knight may have worn a shorter mail shirt known as a *haubergeon*, for this style came into fashion about 1320. Fastened to the sleeves of the hauberk were the besagews and the plates forming the defence for the arm or *vambrace*. Over the hauberk went a coat of plates and to top it all a surcoat or perhaps a handsome padded garment of deco-

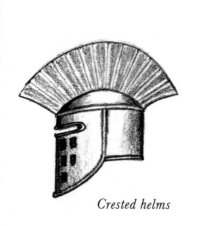

Crested helms

rated silk known as the *gambeson*. If he wore a surcoat it would have been of the latest style with the front cut off short at the thighs. Two belts were put round his waist, one of which was very elaborate and supported his sword. The very last items he put on were the gauntlets and helmet for once these were on he would begin to feel hot and a little uncomfortable.

The helmet he wore would probably be one of the type known as a *bascinet*. These helmets were all pointed at the crown, but some were tall and reached to the ears whilst others reached down to the shoulders. Nearly all were fitted with a movable face-piece known as a *visor*. Many of the bascinets were worn over the coif but others had an attached mail fringe, known as a *camail* or aventail, which hung down to cover the shoulders. If the knight wore no visor on his bascinet he would also put on his great helm for these were still in common use, but were now more conical in shape and rested on the shoulders and chest. Some of these great helms were fitted with visors whilst others had extra strengthening pieces riveted to the side. A leather lining held the helm in place and this could be adjusted to ensure a comfortable fit. Surmounting the helm was the knight's crest, fashioned from painted leather or whalebone and laced on to the helm.

It is likely that he also wore two *ailettes* on his shoulders. These decorated pieces of leather or parchment were usually square in shape although some were round, cross-shaped or diamond. Their purpose was almost certainly heraldic, for by now the use of badges, crests and coats of arms was fairly widespread.

Many knights fearing the loss of their weapons or helmet in battle had guard chains fitted to the helm and to the hilts of the sword and dagger. The other end of the chain was fastened to the belt of the surcoat or to staples on the cuirass. Taking his lance of ash which measured about fourteen feet in length the knight was now ready for battle, or perhaps for the tournament.

Tournaments were really only practice wars and although they were supposed to be friendly affairs tempers were lost, accidents happened and sometimes they developed into small but serious battles with heavy casualties. Many attempts were made to stop them but with little success, and in 1316 the Church withdrew the order that had officially forbidden them. Groups of knights would charge from opposite ends of a field and meet in combat at the centre. This group fighting was known as the *mêlée*, but if the combat took place between only two opponents it was known as a *joust*. From the thirteenth century there were two forms—Jousts of Peace were fought with blunted weapons and the object was to splinter the lance or unhorse your opponent, but Jousts of War were fought with sharp weapons and ended with the wounding or death of one contestant.

The armourer had a demanding job, for although it was not difficult simply to cover the body with plates it was not easy to do so and still allow the wearer to move freely. Some parts of the body like the elbows, knees and armpits were very awkward to protect and here the armourer needed all his skill and ingenuity. A well-designed armour was not only thick enough to prevent a weapon piercing it, but was also made so that the shape of the plate guided a point harmlessly aside.

Knights of the early fourteenth century

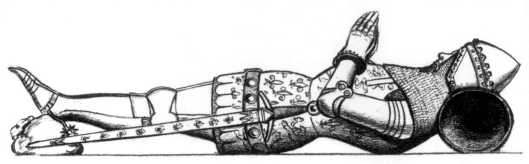

Effigy on the tomb of the Black Prince in Canterbury Cathedral

As early as the middle of the thirteenth century the armourer had been combining the small strips of metal used in the coat of plates into larger pieces. By the 1380s their rounded shape suggests that the breastplate was now fairly solid and we know it was made of several wide strips joined together. It seems quite likely that by the early 1400s the backplate was being made in a similar way.

Leg-pieces were more elaborate and by the 1370s the cuisse, or thigh-piece, which had been made of mail or reinforced padded material was now made of plate. Poleyns were more flexible for they now had several plates and were fitted with a small wing which gave extra protection to the back of the knee. A loop at the top of the cuisse was secured by a leather thong to the belt and this gave support to the whole leg armour of cuisse, poleyn, greave and sabaton.

Sabatons were made from strips of metal which arched over the foot and overlapped one another in such a way that the foot was still able to bend easily. There were no plates on the sole of the foot but just two straps to hold the sabaton in place.

Arms, like the legs, were now completely covered in plate for the upper and lower sections of the arm-pieces were joined by a couter, or elbow-piece, which also had wings of various sizes and shapes.

Sabatons of the fourteenth/early fifteenth century

Strips, or lames, crossed the shoulders and the armpit was covered by a round plate, or besagew. By the beginning of the fifteenth century a larger piece of shoulder armour, the *pauldron*, was being used.

Gauntlets were made of several large plates, and by the 1350s a single large plate was moulded to guard the sides and back of the hand whilst the fingers and thumb were protected by small plates riveted to an inside leather glove. The narrow shape at the wrist has caused this style to be known as an hour-glass gauntlet. Across the back of the gauntlet, one on each of the knuckles, was a row of spikes, and although these *gadlings* were mainly decorative they could, in an emergency, serve as a knuckle-duster.

Helmets were much more elaborate and very graceful in shape, and by about 1330 the bascinet had been extended and now covered the base of the neck and cheeks. From the rim of the bascinet an aventail, or curtain of mail, extended to

Visored bascinets, c. 1390–1400

cover the shoulders. This mail was fastened to the helmet by staples which fitted through a series of holes on the rim and were then secured by a leather thong passed through the staples. Most bascinets were fitted with a visor which was pivoted either at the brow or else at the side. The visors were of many shapes and sizes, but the most striking was that which tapered to a point—often called a pig-faced bascinet. A number of holes allowed some fresh air to the wearer who peered out through two slits carefully protected by flanges. Visors were easily removed by withdrawing two pins at the side. Inside the helmet there was plenty of padding which was stuffed with grass, horsehair or similar materials.

If the bascinet was not fitted with a visor it was possible to wear the great helm as well but, in fact, fewer knights were wearing the great helm in battle. If used for jousting or the tournament the helms were secured to the cuirass by great *hasps* or *charnels*. Late in the fourteenth century a special form of great helm, the frog-mouthed helm, was developed and this has a sight which was clear only when the body and helm were tilted forward. If the knight leaned back the opening was so placed that no spear could possibly enter.

Beneath all the plate armour the aketon was still being worn as well as a haubergeon which reached only to the hips and elbows.

The long flowing surcoat had now gone out of the fashion and had been replaced by a shorter padded *jupon* on which was often displayed the wearer's coat of arms.

During the fifteenth century certain towns became famous for their fine-quality armour. In Northern Italy the greatest centre was probably Milan which had been producing armour

Fighting sword, c. 1415

for export as early as the thirteenth century. In Germany the towns of Nuremberg, Innsbruck, Landshut and Augsburg were also producing armour. Each area tended to develop its own style—Italy produced a rather round, smooth style whilst the German armours tended to be rather more spiky in appearance. Fifteenth-century armour was light, efficient, graceful and beautiful in its own right and some of the finest ever made.

Knight—second half of fourteenth century

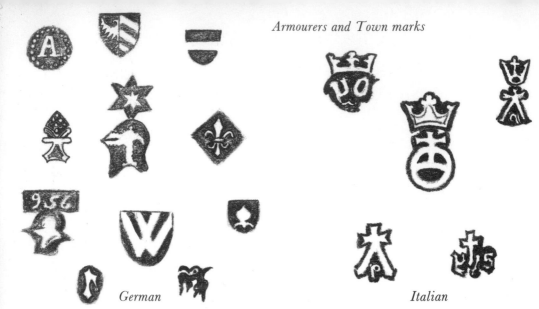

German   *Italian*

Armour craftsmen kept much of their craft secret so that our knowledge of their methods is rather limited, but we do know that most of the shaping was done when the metal was cold. Straightforward hammering was done by water-driven hammers, but most of the shaping was done by hand over a metal block or stake. As the craftsmen formed the pieces from single plates they carefully left certain parts thicker than others—a breastplate was thick at the centre and thinner at the sides—a helmet was thicker on the top and at the front of the skull than at the sides. Between each period of hammering the metal was carefully heated and allowed to cool since hammering made the metal hard and brittle. Special armours were made to measure and decorated according to the customer's wishes, and when the order was completed the master armourer often had his personal mark stamped on the armour. A town mark was also added to show that the workmanship was up to standard.

Fifteenth-century war hammer and mace
(from Wallace Collection—London)

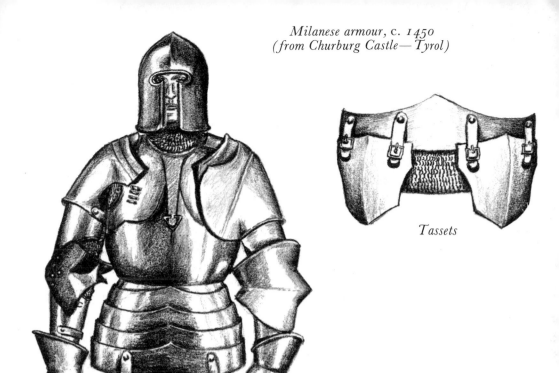

Milanese armour, c. 1450
(from Churburg Castle—Tyrol)

Tassets

Italian armour of the fifteenth century was rounded in shape and had breastplates made of two separate pieces fastened together by a single strap at the centre. Backplates had three or four overlapping lames. From the bottom of the breastplate hung the skirt or *fauld*, and from this hung two plates to protect the thighs. These *tassets* varied in shape, being nearly triangular during the second half of the century. Pauldrons were big and sometimes overlapped each other at the back. Since knights used their right arm to swing their swords most right pauldrons were smaller than those on the left. Sometimes the top of the pauldron was extended to give extra protection for the neck and these projections are known as *haute-pieces*.

Mail was still worn under the armour and the Italians frequently used mail rather than plate to form the skirt of the armour.

Gothic armour—Augsburg, c. 1480

There was another group of helmets made in a variety of shapes, although all were called *sallets*. Some were very simple and rather like earlier bascinets whilst others had reinforcing plates fastened to the brow. Most had a visor as well as a pointed 'tail' to cover the back of the neck.

Early in the fifteenth century the style of helmet known as an *armet* appeared, and this form developed from the bascinet. Armets had a distinguishing feature in that the cheek-pieces were hinged at the top and lifted upwards. Cheek-pieces were deep and overlapped at the front when closed, although they left a clear open space at the top for the wearer to see through. By the middle of the century most had a reinforcing plate above the brow and a detachable visor. At the back, level with the neck, was a metal peg with a large flat disc or *rondel* on top. This rondel was probably there to protect a strap which held in place a *wrapper* or plate worn to give extra protection to the face.

German armourers had also developed their own special styles during the fifteenth century and about 1460 they began producing some of their most attractive armours in the style usually called Gothic. Its general appearance is slim, somewhat spiky but most graceful. Helmets are usually sallets, frequently with a long pointed tail and a *bevor* or throat guard. Cuirasses are slender with a short fauld, or skirt, and like the Italian armours often have a mail skirt. Breastplates were still being made of several pieces, but by the end of the fifteenth century many were now shaped from a single plate. Thigh defences were frequently made of several horizontal strips and at the top was a raised ridge to prevent a weapon sliding under the armour. Poleyns usually had only a small wing. The greaves were slim and fastened to the sabatons which were steel copies of civilian shoes with long toes, sometimes so long that they were detachable to enable the wearer to walk. Spurs had very long necks and a rowel shaped like a star. Arms were protected by graceful vambraces and pauldrons, whilst the gauntlets were made with long pointed cuffs.

Most Gothic armours had the edges cut into graceful curves and points which were sometimes edged with brass. All the surfaces of the plates were decorated with raised ridges which gave a little extra strength and also helped to deflect an enemy's weapon.

Armour was intended for use and not just for show and every piece was carefully designed and fashioned with this purpose in mind. Weight was kept down as far as was possible and here we must clear up one very common mistake about armour. Many comics, films and books suggest that if a knight fell from his horse he lay helpless because the armour held him down. A complete field harness weighed about five stone—about the same as a young child and this weight was distributed over the body. Now you can see that just as it is ridiculous to suggest that a child could hold down a trained fighting man it is silly to

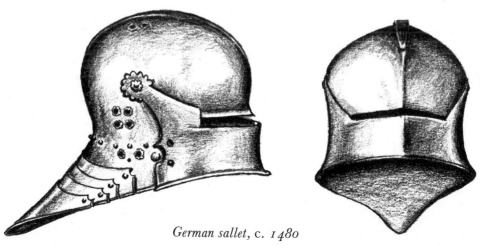

German sallet, c. *1480*

36

think that armour would keep a man pinned to the ground. Trained warriors were proud of being able to vault into the saddle of their horse when completely armed. We do not have to rely on boasts of long-dead soldiers, for complete and genuine fifteenth- and sixteenth-century armours have been worn by men with no previous experience and they were able to stand up, lie down, jump, run, mount and dismount with little or no difficulty. It has also been said that knights were hoisted into the saddle by cranes and this is also quite wrong. The very heaviest armours for the tilt weighed only about one hundred pounds, or just over seven stone and the only help that the tilter needed to mount, even wearing such heavy armour, was probably a mounting-block.

Armour manufacture was probably at its peak during the sixteenth century, but from then on there was a gradual decline in design and usefulness. During the fifteenth and sixteenth centuries armour was considered a necessity for all knights and cost a great deal of money. It was often the gift of princes who might give a *garniture* consisting of a complete field harness, tilting armour and horse armour, a total of some sixty pieces. Armourers were treated with the respect that their skill deserved and it was not uncommon for one famous armourer to produce only for his sovereign.

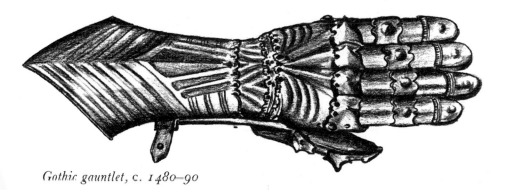

Gothic gauntlet, c. 1480–90

As plate armour became more complex it became almost impossible for a knight to arm himself and an assistant was essential, usually a squire who was himself hoping to become a knight. First he helped the knight put on an arming doublet which was a padded tunic fitted with a collar and skirt of mail as well as sections stitched to those places, elbows and armpits, difficult to cover with plate. A number of laces were attached to the doublet and these were used to tie on or support various pieces of armour. Now the arming started from the feet and legs with sabatons, greaves, poleyns and cuisses strapped carefully into position. Next came the *gorget*, or metal collar, which locked by means of a turning pin which passed through a keyhole-shaped slot and then turned, or else was secured by a spring clip. Breastplate and backplate were now strapped in place and next came the arm-pieces. Gauntlets and helmets were last of all to be put on and effigies show the gauntlets tied together and hanging over the dagger sheath until needed.

Often horses had their own armour or *bards*. At first it was a covering of quilted cloth or mail with a metal plate for the front of the head—the *chamfron*. In the thirteenth century, plates of leather or metal replaced the mail to cover the chest (*peytral*), sides (*flanchards*), back (*crupper*) and neck (*crinet*). Bards were abandoned from the mid sixteenth century, although the chamfron was still used as late as the 1630s.

As armour became stronger and more effective in warding off blows, swords were used more for thrusting at poorly protected parts of the body. This change started during the thirteenth century and by the middle of the fourteenth century

German hand-and-a-half sword, early sixteenth century

swords were being made with blades designed entirely for thrusting, and a century later there appeared the *estoc* with little or no edge at all but a stiff thick pointed blade.

Some swords were made with grips that were long enough to be held in one hand or in both hands to give a harder blow, and these are known as hand and a half swords. Bigger swords, so large that they could only be used with two hands, were made as early as the 1350s but they were not common until the sixteenth century.

Pommels altered in design over the centuries for the tea-cosy type disappeared about the middle of the twelfth century but the brazil-nut type continued until the late thirteenth century. Many pommels were circular and flat and this style was in use as early as the middle of the twelfth century. The rim of the wheel was shaved off to give a sloping edge in the thirteenth century, but towards the end of the fifteenth century had once again become flat and rather thick.

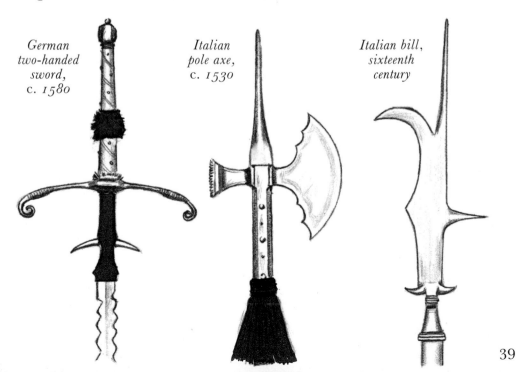

German two-handed sword, c. 1580

Italian pole axe, c. 1530

Italian bill, sixteenth century

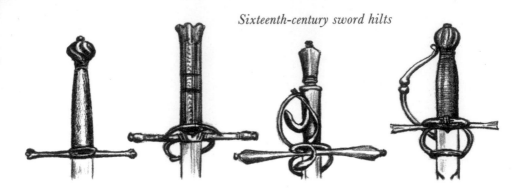

Guards or quillons were, at first, straight, but about 1400 an extra bar was added to protect the first finger, for this was often hooked over the quillon to give a better grip. The top few inches of the blade were left blunt, the *ricasso*, so that there was no danger of cutting this finger. Rings were added to the sides of the quillons about the middle of the fifteenth century and a guard, or knuckle-bow, went from the quillons to the pommel.

Sheaths were made from thin strips of wood which were fastened together and covered with a layer of leather, or parchment, or rich material. The tip of the sheath was protected by a metal cap or *chape*.

Sword belts were often elaborate and decorative with the sheath laced on, but about 1250 they were designed to carry the sheath so that it hung at an angle. The belt was in two pieces, each of which was laced to the sheath and then buckled at the front. At the beginning of the fourteenth century sheaths were attached to the belt by rings fixed to metal *lockets*, or bands, on the sheath. About the middle of the fourteenth century the belt was worn straight across the hips and sword and dagger were hooked on, but in the middle of the fifteenth century rings were again in use.

Early lances were simply ordinary spears with a long wooden shaft of ash some ten to fourteen feet long, but from early in the

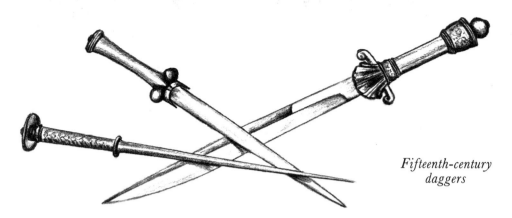

fourteenth century a metal disc, or *vamplate*, was fitted round
the shaft just in front of the hand. The shaft was also often
thickened just in front of the hand to ensure a firmer grip for,
as you can imagine, it was no easy task to manage one of these
long lances. When the lance hit its target it was pushed back
under the arm and to stop this a bracket, or lance-rest, was
fitted to the breastplate. The lance-rest engaged with a disc
fitted behind the grip on the lance. For Jousts of Peace the
sharp head was replaced by a blunt, three-pronged head. For
fifteenth-century jousts in which the idea was simply to splinter
a lance, special light hollow lances were made.

The longbow was at its peak during the latter part of the
fourteenth and early fifteenth centuries and its arrows were
feared by even the best-armoured knights. Bow staves were
nearly six feet long with a diameter of several inches at the
centre and the best were made of foreign yew, although other
woods were used. Strings were of hemp, flax or silk and were
only fitted into place when action was imminent. Horn tips,
or notches cut into the staff, held the string in place and a great
deal of strength was required to bend the bow with its eighty-
pound pull.

Arrows were of ash, birch and even oak with goose, or more
rarely, peacock feathers. In the hands of a trained archer these

iron-tipped shafts would pierce a four-inch-thick oak door or pin a man to his horse. Greatest range was probably about 350 to 400 yards, but a great deal of practice was needed to become proficient in its use and send an aimed shaft this distance.

Crossbows were now even more powerful, for early in the fourteenth century a composite bow fashioned from layers of wood and horn was used. About 1315 a steel bow, stronger still, was adopted and the weapon was now so difficult to span or pull back that the archer was unable to do so by hand. The *windlass* and *cranequin* were used and these both worked by winding a handle which operated pulleys and gears to wind back the cord. In the sixteenth century a simpler and ingenious double lever, called a *goat's foot* appeared. Its very power made the crossbow slow to load and discharge and an archer using a longbow could loose off several shafts whilst the crossbow was firing one.

Maces were common and varied only in the design of the heads which ranged from single solid blocks to graceful flanges on the Gothic mace.

For foot combat most of these weapons were used as well as a number of pole arms or staff weapons such as the *poleaxe, bill, halberd* and *partisan.*

So far we have not mentioned firearms, but by the fifteenth century they were beginning to play a more and more important part in the art of war. In the fourteenth century cannons were used largely for sieges and were looked on as dangerous and unreliable weapons, but the introduction of small handguns had changed this attitude and armourers began to think about making their armours strong enough to stop a bullet.

Billman and Longbowman
late fourteenth/early fifteenth century

43

German and Italian armourers continued to experiment and produced styles which differed and other craftsmen still tended to copy these styles. In 1515 Henry VIII set up his own royal armour workshops at Greenwich, just outside London. German and Dutch armourers started the workshops and although the armour they produced was at first more like the Italian style, Greenwich armour soon had its own special features. It was usually good quality, decorated and had a wide-shouldered appearance because of the rather large pauldrons. At first the workshops produced armours only for the King and his personal friends and they were therefore highly decorated with etching, engraving and gilding.

One of the characteristic styles of the early-sixteenth-century armour, especially in Germany, is the so-called Maximilian. This is easy to recognise for the whole surface, except for the greaves, is covered with raised ridges or fluting which not only gave extra strength but also helped to deflect blows. Early examples of this style tend to have less fluting, but all have the rather puffed breastplate.

Italian cinquedea, c. 1500

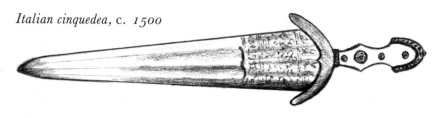

Swiss Holbein dagger, 1573

44

Maximilian armour, c. 1520

So great was the armourer's skill that he could fashion metal almost like cloth and many armours were made with the visor in the shape of an animal's head or a grotesque mask. Armours were made to copy the civilian styles with the metal worked into folds and pleats. Other armours were decorated with patterns hammered out so that the shapes stood up above the surface. Embossing, as it is called, was beautiful and difficult to do, but it was not good design since the raised decoration prevented a sword edge, or lance point, from sliding clear as had happened on the earlier armours. If the armour was intended only for show or parades this was not important, but in war it could be very dangerous. This gradual decline in the design of armour reflected the feeling that it was no longer quite so important as in the past and this change was again caused by the ever-increasing power of firearms. Armour was no longer quite so protective as it had been and a bullet fired from a handgun could kill a knight who had spent a large sum of money on his armour. The armourer tried to produce armour in attractive forms so that his customers would still buy even though they realised it was no longer quite so necessary.

Although armour for the battlefield might be declining that for the tilt was certainly not and the sixteenth century saw some of the finest tilting armour ever made. Some armours were sold which were a kind of do-it-yourself kit for the basic harness was for the field, but a series of double pieces could be added to convert it to a tilting armour for one or more of the many jousts.

Jousting was now a complicated sport with many rules and different courses. Some were still run in open fields but from about 1420 it became more common to have a fence down the centre of the field with the contestants placed on opposite sides. This arrangement reduced the chances of the horses colliding.

In most jousts the object was to unhorse your opponent or to splinter your lance with a good direct hit. Marks were awarded for the various hits, a difficult one on the helmet scored more than one to the body, and the highest scorer was judged the winner. Prizes were given such as a diamond for first place, a ruby for second and a sapphire for third place.

Armour for the joust, mid sixteenth century

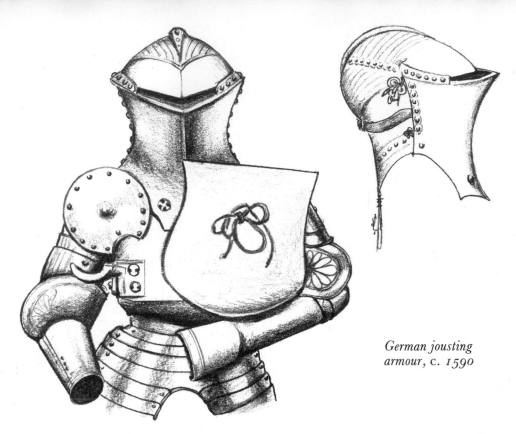

German jousting armour, c. 1590

Ordinary field armour was not used for jousting early after the sixteenth century and special armours were designed. Frequently these jousting armours have no leg defences since the fence and a specially designed saddle both gave protection. In Germany especially, different styles of armour were worn according to whether blunt or·sharpened lances were used. For use with the blunt lance the armour included a frog-mouthed helm, special arm-pieces and a small wooden shield hanging on the left shoulder. During the sixteenth century the helm was replaced by a sturdy close helmet which was bolted

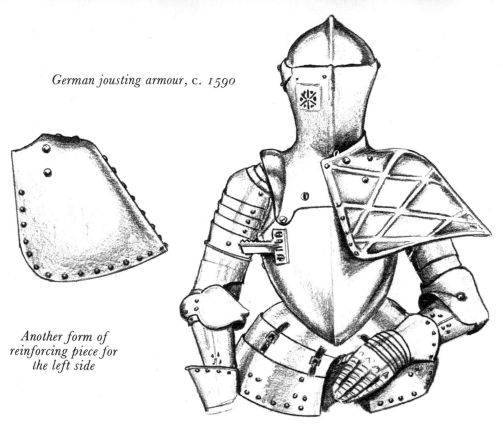

German jousting armour, c. 1590

Another form of reinforcing piece for the left side

on to the cuirass and a metal shield replaced the wooden one. Armours intended for jousts using a sharp lance usually had a sallet and a great reinforcing piece which covered the entire left side of the rider. To help steady the rather unwieldy lance a bar or *queue* was fixed on the right-hand side of the armour. Despite all these extra defences accidents still happened; Henry II of France lost his life in 1559 and Henry VIII of England nearly suffered the same fate in 1524 when the Duke of Suffolk splintered a lance on his helmet whilst the King's visor was still raised.

50   Landsknecht

Officer in black-and-white armour

Foot combats were also popular and all kinds of weapons such as swords, clubs, daggers and poleaxes were used. Some were fought over the tilt, others took the form of a general mêlée. Special foot combat armours were designed, often with a very wide skirt or *tonlet*.

Tournaments and jousts gradually fell from fashion and by the middle of the seventeenth century were quite forgotten in England although in other countries they survived in simple form until much later. The last great tournament in England took place in 1839 when Lord Eglinton decided to revive the ancient glory of Chivalry. Unfortunately, it poured with rain and the amateur and inexpert jousters merely looked rather silly.

Mention has been made of a close helmet for this appeared during the sixteenth century and differed from the armet in one important point. In place of the armet's cheek-pieces hinged at the top, the close helmet had a visor and bevor pivoted at the side. When putting on the helmet both pieces were raised and when in position the bevor was lowered and locked in place whilst the visor could be left open or closed as desired. A further change took place about 1540 when the visor was made in two pieces. Some close helmets were designed to lock on to the rim of the gorget so that the head could rotate but could not tilt backwards or forwards.

German close helmet, c. *1530*

German armet, c. *1540*

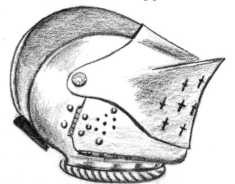

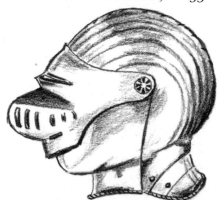

Burgonet, late sixteenth century

Burgonet with buffe, late sixteenth century

Frequent wars in the sixteenth century had created a demand for armour for the ordinary troops who had previously worn quilted armour, odd pieces picked up from the battlefield or cheap versions of good-quality pieces. Some had worn *brigandines* which had dozens of plates riveted to a jacket whilst others had cheaper *jacks* where the plates were stitched in place. From the early sixteenth century many bodies of troops were issued with *corselets* which were light half armours with a collar or gorget, cuirass, vambraces, gauntlets, tassets to the knee and some light open-faced helmet. One cheap corselet, costing sixteen shillings in 1512, was known as an Almain Rivet.

Frequently worn with the corselet was the *burgonet* which fitted fairly closely to the head and had a high comb, a peak but no visor. Some burgonets were, however, supplied with a face-piece or *buffe* which could be strapped on to the helmet. About the middle of the century some burgonets were fitted with a sliding nasal, or bar, passing through the peak.

Morions were light helmets made in a variety of shapes often with a high comb and a narrow brim—a type also known as a *cabasset*.

*Italian comb morion,
late sixteenth century*

*Cabasset,
late sixteenth century*

*English pot helmet,
mid seventeenth century*

*Halberd,
early sixteenth century*

*Pikemen,
early seventeenth century*

53

The late sixteenth and early seventeenth centuries saw the tide begin to turn against the armourer. More powerful weapons were changing the ways of war which was becoming so fast moving that heavily armoured, slow-moving armies were useless. Firearms were becoming plentiful, more reliable and far more deadly so that to resist the bullet, armour had to be so thick that it was too heavy to wear with comfort. Armour had been proved, i.e. tested, by discharging crossbow bolts against it, but from the sixteenth century firearms replaced the crossbow. Armour was described as pistol, caliver (a light musket) or musket proof, and if you look at armour in museums you can often see the dent made by the bullet when the armour was being proved. Not every piece of armour was proved, usually only the breast, back and helmet were done. Since these pieces had to be made heavier soldiers tended to leave off the less important parts of the armour to reduce the overall weight. Leg-pieces were among the first to go and heavy cavalry now wore three-quarter, or cuirassier's, armour. These armours, often rather ugly, had a thick, close helmet and tassets which reached only to the knee, the rest of the leg being protected by thick leather boots. Many cuirassiers changed their close helmets for burgonets, whilst light cavalry left off all armour except for an open helmet, gorgets, pauldrons and cuirass. The left hand and forearm was protected by a bridle gauntlet which had a long cuff reaching right to the elbow and was held in place by a leather flap which fastened to a button on the sleeve.

Foot soldiers too were discarding their armour and many replaced it with a buff leather coat which was made from ox-hide treated with oil. These coats had an off-white or yellow, rather fluffy, look, but were strong enough to turn a

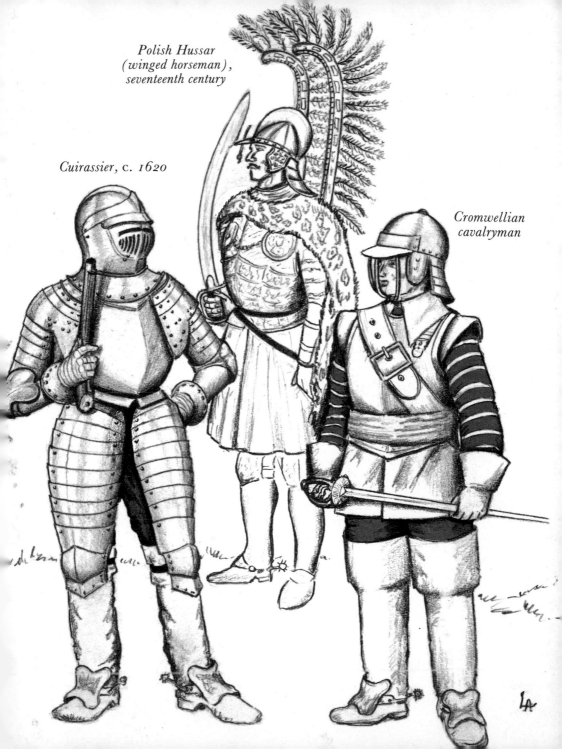

*Polish Hussar
(winged horseman),
seventeenth century*

Cuirassier, c. 1620

*Cromwellian
cavalryman*

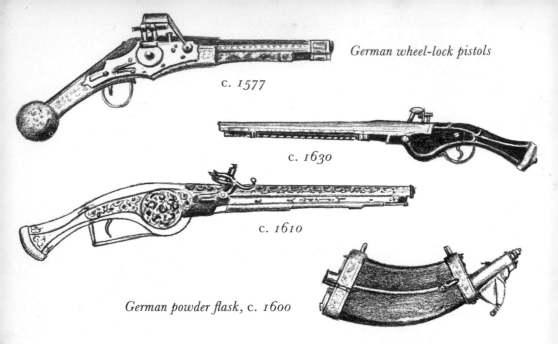

German wheel-lock pistols

c. *1577*

c. *1630*

c. *1610*

German powder flask, c. *1600*

sword cut although they would not, of course, stop a bullet. Buff coats were also adopted by the cavalry and were commonly worn during the Civil War in England.

Against the cavalry stood the pikemen armed with a long spear or pike which might be anything up to twenty feet long. Their job was to protect the musketeers whilst they were re-loading and they were more heavily armoured than most with a large, wide-brimmed helmet called a *pot*, a collar or gorget, breastplate and backplate and *tassets*. The tassets were made in one piece although rivets were applied to make it appear as if they were in fact made up from strips like the earlier ones.

*Italian left-hand
dagger*, c. *1600*

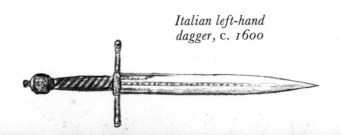

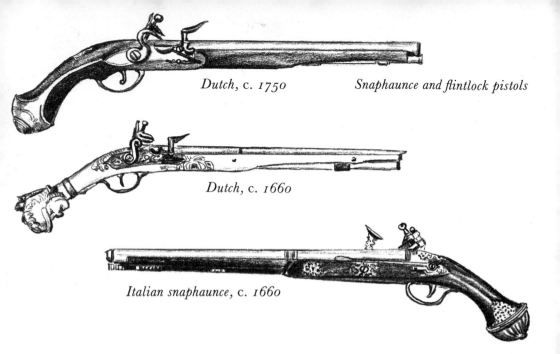

Dutch, c. *1750*

Snaphaunce and flintlock pistols

Dutch, c. *1660*

Italian snaphaunce, c. *1660*

Weapons, too, had undergone great changes during the sixteenth and seventeenth centuries for firearms were now far more plentiful and the cavalry had largely abandoned the lance relying on pistol and sword. Swords altered only slightly until the beginning of the sixteenth century, but from then on there were great changes, especially in the hilt. Extra loops and bars were added and soon the hand was almost entirely enclosed. As armour was discarded swords were designed for thrusting as well as slashing and schools of fencing, designed to teach the latest methods of fighting with the sword, sprang up especially in Italy. Swords for thrusting and slashing were known as rapiers, but from the mid sixteenth century those rapiers with

Spanish cup-hilt
for a rapier,
c. *1650*

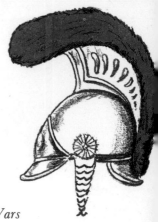

English and French cavalry helmets—Napoleonic Wars

no cutting edge and relying solely on the point were known as *tucks*. Rapiers were frequently very long and were often used with a dagger, held in the left hand, which was used to parry or push aside an enemy's blade.

Blades were shortened about the 1630s and in Spain appeared the cup-hilt rapier. These have a shell guard which replaced some of the loops of the swept-hilt rapier. These rapiers tended to become shorter and lighter whilst the guards were simplified and about the middle of the seventeenth century we get the first of the small swords. These delicate, deadly swords had two small, shaped shells, a knuckle-bow and two loops with a very short quillon at the rear. Beautifully made, often with hilts of silver, these little swords, with some changes, remained in fashion until late in the eighteenth century when swords were no longer worn.

Small swords were civilian swords and military swords are broader, heavier and much less elaborate. Basket-hilted broadswords were common for cavalry use and are often known as *claymores*, although the true claymore was a great two-handed sword used by the Scots and Irish.

British infantry officer's sword—1796 pattern

From the latter part of the eighteenth century it became common practice to issue swords to the army or at least lay down rules as to what type of sword they should have and these are known as regulation swords. Since many officers interpreted the orders in different ways, in fact, these swords often varied quite a lot.

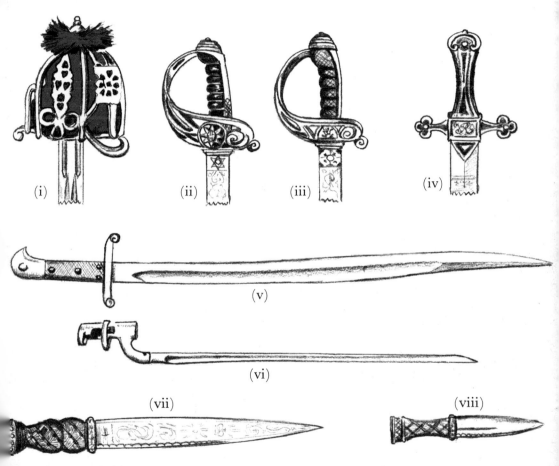

British infantry weapons—Dress Regulations of 1865
(i) *Highland officer's sword,* (ii) *Guards officer's sword,* (iii) *Rifle regiment officer's sword,* (iv) *Rifle regiment bugler's sword,* (v) *Sword bayonet,* (vi) *Bayonet,* (vii) *Highland dirk,* (viii) *Highland* skean dhu

Cavalry were now armed only with firearms and swords whilst the infantry had a musket, bayonet and sword although most of the swords, except for officers, were withdrawn from the infantry in 1768. Officers also carried a short spear-like weapon known as a *spontoon* until 1786, but sergeants continued to carry it until 1830.

After the Civil War in England armour was used less and less until only the cavalry retained its cuirass and this last item vanished by the early eighteenth century when they were returned to store. Other countries retained armour for their cavalry and the French were still using theirs at the beginning of the First World War.

*English
infantry
officer
c. 1758*

*Prussian Hussar,
c. 1763*

Some armour was reintroduced in 1820 by George IV when the Household Cavalry were issued with helmets and cuirasses, but these were essentially for use on parade rather than war.

In 1830 vanished the last lingering remnant of armour, for in that year officers discarded their gorgets. By this time these gorgets had shrunk to small half-moon plates hung upon a chain about the officer's neck and were really only a badge or mark of rank.

Royal Horse Guard,
c. *1860*

German Garde du
Corps *Kurassier,*
c. *1912*

In 1914 the First World War broke out in Europe and soon the armourers were hard at work again, for trench warfare resulted in a large number of head wounds and it became apparent that some special protection was needed. The French were the first to experiment with steel helmets—tin hats the soldiers called them—but it is interesting to know that the German helmet was supposed to have been designed with the medieval sallet in mind. By 1916 most of the armies engaged in the war were being issued with some form of helmet.

Another phase of armoured warfare was ushered in by the appearance of the tank in 1916 and the imaginative use of the caterpillar track and armour was to change the whole style of war.

Modern armies, navies and air forces all use armour to protect their tanks, troop carriers, ships and pilots. New materials such as plastics are used and great machines have replaced the craftsman, but in some ways the craft is just the same. Bullet-proof waistcoats worn by police and politicians are still made in much the same way as the old scale armour.

Our look at arms and armour has only been concerned with Europe, but in Africa and Asia armour was used although it was often fashioned, not from metal, but from shells, skins or even vines. Mail was used by many African and Indian races right through the nineteenth century and Japan produced some very elaborate and striking armour as well as some of the finest swords in the world.

Steel helmets of World War I

French *British* *German*

Visit your local museum or one of the big collections of arms and armour and with a little effort you can imagine the neighing of horses, the shouts, the colour and the horror of war. Man has spent much of his history in warfare and however much we may disapprove and regret this terrible story it is still part of our heritage.

Modern British soldier

*Anglo-Saxon Huscare,
c. 1066*

INDEX